PHP:

Learn PHP in 24 Hours or Less

A Beginner's Guide To Learning PHP Programming Now

Table of Contents

Introduction

In this book you will find detailed instructions on how to learn the basics of the PHP language.

This eBook will explain what PHP is and how it can help you in building web applications. Aside from giving theoretical explanations, this book will provide you with actual codes and practical examples. You will be able to learn this computer language quickly even if you have never programmed anything before. If you're looking for a comprehensive reference for PHP, this is the book you need.

By reading this book, you will be able to:

- Learn the fundamental elements of PHP

- Know the syntax that you should use while writing PHP scripts

- Create your own variables and constants

- Call the built-in methods and functions of PHP

- Handle errors and exceptions in your web applications

- Receive and store user inputs securely

- Master the basics of OOP (i.e. object-oriented programming)

- Create classes and subclasses

- Know the connection between PHP and MySQL

PHP is an excellent scripting language. It can help you create robust websites and web applications. If you want to be an effective PHP user in just 24 hours, read this book carefully.

Let's begin the journey.

Chapter 1: PHP – The Basics

The PHP language (i.e. PHP: Hypertext Processor) borrows some of its syntaxes from other programming languages (e.g. C, Perl, Java, etc.). People consider PHP as a hybrid computer language, acquiring the best functionalities of other languages and forming a powerful and intuitive scripting language.

In this chapter, you'll learn about the fundamental aspects of PHP such as variables, comments, and language structure. Read this material carefully if you want to be an effective PHP user.

HTML Embedding

You'll use PHP to create dynamic webpages. Thus, you should know how to embed it into the most popular scripting language: HTML (i.e. HyperText Markup Language). Check the following code:

<HTML>

<HEAD> This is a sample. </HEAD>

<BODY>

This code wants to greet you:

<?php

print "Hi, how are you?";

```
?>
```

```
</BODY>
</HTML>
```

This example shows you how to embed PHP snippets into HTML codes. Each time the language interpreter encounters the "open" tag of PHP (i.e. <?php), it executes the embedded code until it reaches the "close" tag (i.e. ?>). Here, PHP will replace the PHP snippet with the appropriate output (if any) and pass the non-PHP code (e.g. HTML) to the user's website client. If you will run the code given above, your screen will show you this:

```
<HTML>
<HEAD> This is a sample. </HEAD>
<BODY>
```

This code wants to greet you:

Hi, how are you?

```
</BODY>
</HTML>
```

Comments

You also need to learn how to add comments to your PHP codes. As a programmer, you will use comments to add details and descriptions to your work without affecting its output and behavior. The PHP language supports three methods of commenting. These methods are:

- The "Shell" Method (i.e. #) - In this method, you'll begin your comments with the hashtag symbol. This symbol only works for single-line comments. For example:

  # This comment is awesome.

- The "C" Method (e.g. /* */) - This method is taken from the C language. This option allows you to create multi-line comments. For instance:

  / This comment*

  spans

  *multiple lines. */*

- The "C++" Method (i.e. //) - Use this method when writing a single-line comment. Here's an example:

- *// This is a sample.*

Variables

The variables used in PHP are different from those of compiled languages (e.g. C, C++, Java, etc.). This difference lies in the fact that PHP variables are "weakly typed." Simply put, PHP allows you to use variables even without prior declaration. You don't have to declare variables explicitly or assign their type. Thus, you can change the data type of your variables whenever you want.

In the PHP language, you should introduce your variables using the dollar sign (i.e. $). You can use letters, numbers, and underscores when naming your variables. However, you can't use a number as the first character of a variable's name. That means $one_apple is valid while $1_apple isn't.

As mentioned earlier, PHP lets you use undeclared variables. The examples given below will illustrate this idea:

$PI = 3.14159;

$radius = 10;

This code created two variables without declaring their data type. Here, "PI" belongs to the floating-point type while "radius" belongs to the integer type.

Important Note: The PHP language is not compatible with global variables. Each variable is local to its scope. If it is created within a function, it will disappear once the function no longer exists.

Indirect Reference

PHP allows you to access a variable using indirect reference. That means you can generate and access a variable by name during runtime. Analyze this example:

```php
$car = "BMW";

$$car = "Z4";

print $car;
```

Your screen will display "Z4" if you will run this code snippet. The second line of this code accesses the variable named "car" and changes its value. As you can see, that line has an extra dollar sign. That sign tells the PHP interpreter that you are referring to the value contained by the variable involved. In this example, a new variable named "Z4" is generated.

Important Note: There are no limits regarding the number of indirect references that you can use. That means you can place any number of dollar signs before a variable's name.

How to Manage Variables

There are three constructs that you can use to manage your PHP variables. These constructs allow you to verify the existence of certain variables, delete variables, and check their truth values. Let's discuss each language construct in detail:

- isset() - This construct checks whether PHP has declared a particular variable. It will give you "true" (i.e. a Boolean value) if your chosen variable already exists; otherwise, it will give you false. The script given below will illustrate this concept:

if (isset ($my_name)) {

*   print '$my_name exists';*

}

  If the variable named "my_name" exists, your screen will display "$my_name exists." If your code doesn't have that variable, however, you won't get any output.

- unset() - Use this construct to "undeclare" an existing variable. If there are no references that point to the variable's value, the memory assigned to it will become freed up. Invoking isset() on a variable that you've deleted gives you "false." Here's an example:

$gameconsole = "PlayStation 4";

unset ($gameconsole);

if (isset ($gameconsole)) {

    print '$gameconsole exists';

}

Important Note: You can also use unset() and isset() on object properties and array elements (you'll learn about these later). The syntax that you should use is:

☐ For object properties:

☐ *if (isset ($object – property)) { ... }*

☐ For array elements:

☐ *if isset ($array ["offset"})) { ... }*

- empty() - With this construct, you can check whether a variable exists or is set to false. While checking the truth value of a variable, empty() will convert the data into Boolean and checks whether it is true or false. Check the following script:

```
if (empty ($gameconsole)) {

    print 'Sorry, this variable doesn't have a value';

}
```

The Superglobal Variables

In general, you can't use global variables (i.e. variables that you can access from any part of your code) in PHP. However, this scripting language has built-in variables that act like typical global variables. These variables, known   as superglobals, are one of the best tools that you can use while writing PHP scripts. Here are some of the superglobals that you will encounter:

- $_ENV[] - This is an array that contains environment variables.

- $_GET[] - This array holds all of the "GET" variables gathered from the user's web browser.

- $_POST[] - This superglobal is similar to $_GET. The only difference is that $_POST involves POST variables only.

- $_SERVER – This kind of array holds the values of web-server variables.

The Data Types

The PHP language supports eight data types. Five of these data types are scalar. The remaining three, however, has unique properties that differentiate them from others. As mentioned earlier, a PHP variable can hold any data type. Keep in mind that PHP variables behave according to the type of data they hold. Here are the data types that you will encounter while using PHP:

Integers

An integer is a whole number and has the same range as the "long" data type of C. In most machines (e.g. Intel Pentium processors), an integer is a 32-bit signed number that can be as low as -2,147,483,648 or as high as 2,147,483,647.

You may write an integer in octal (with zero as a prefix), in decimal (without any prefix), and in hexadecimal form (with 0x as a prefix). Additionally, PHP integers can be positive or negative. Here are some examples of valid PHP integers:

- 30000

- 0xCDEF

- 003

- -90

Floating-Point Numbers

A floating-point number, also called real number, is PHP's own version of the C language's "double" type. When accessed using a typical platform, a floating-point number is 8 bytes in size and can reach as high as 1.8E+308 down to 2.2E-308. In general, a floating-point value can have an exponent, a decimal point, and "+" or "-" sign. The list given below shows some valid floating-point numbers:

- 65.7E43

- -1800.4

- +0.8e-3

String

In PHP, strings are sequences of characters (i.e. letters and numbers) that are null-terminated all the time. Unlike other computer languages, however, PHP remembers the length of a string internally rather than relying on the null terminator. This approach allows the PHP interpreter to handle binary information easily. For instance, you can use this function to generate images on-the-fly and send it to a web browser. The largest size a string can have depends on the C compiler and computer that you're using. However, you can be sure it can handle 2GB of data without any problems.

Important Note: Don't create programs that verify the limit discussed above. You will likely reach the memory limit of your platform first.

While adding a string value to your PHP code, you may use single quotes, double quotes, or here-docs. Let's discuss these options in detail:

- *Single Quotes* – This is the simplest option that you can use when creating a string. Write your string between a pair of quotes. This approach supports two types of escape characters, which are: \' and \\. You will learn about escape characters later.

- *Double Quotes* – This option is more complex than the previous one. You can use this to hold any character. However, when working with a special symbol, you need to use the backslash character. Adding a backslash before a special character is called "escaping." Here are the escape characters that you will encounter while using PHP:

  o \n – Use this to add a newline character to your codes. A newline character is the character you'll get after pressing the Enter key.

  o \t – With this, you can add a tab character to your PHP codes.

  o \\ - You can use this symbol to add a backslash character to your scripts. As you can see, the backslash character is used to activate the special functions of other characters. Thus, you need to type two backslash characters in order to get an ordinary backslash.

- o \" - Double quotes are used to enclose strings. To add a normal double quote character, you need to introduce it using a backslash.

- o \r – This escape symbol allows you to insert a line feed to your PHP script.

- o \$ - Use this symbol to add a normal dollar sign to your codes. As you know, $ is used to create a PHP variable.

- o \0 – With this symbol, you can add the 0 character of ASCII.

- o \{octal number} – Use this to add an ASCII character to your code. Here, you should use the octal representation of the character you want to add.

- o \x{hexadecimal number} – This escape character is almost identical to the octal one. The only difference is that this escape symbol requires the hexadecimal representation of the character.

Another powerful functionality of a double-quoted string is that it can hold the notation of an expression or variable. The samples given below will help you understand how this function works. The system will automatically replace variable references with the value of the variables involved. If the value isn't a string, the system will convert that data into its corresponding string representation (e.g. 999 will be converted to "999").

"The answer is $answer\n"

The $i array offset holds $array[$i]"

In situations where you want to concatenate a string with a value (e.g. an expression or a variable) and its syntax is insufficient, you may use the dot operator (i.e. ".") to combine (or concatenate) multiple strings. You'll learn more about this operator later.

- *Here-Docs* – This option allows you to embed huge pieces of content to your codes. These pieces of content may have single quotes or double quotes. When using the here-docs delimiter, you won't have to worry about escaping your symbols.

Boolean

As mentioned earlier, PHP converts data types automatically. You should know that data types are often converted to Boolean during runtime. That's because in conditional codes (e.g. loops, "if" statements, etc.), the system will convert the data types involved into Boolean to see whether they satisfy the given condition. In addition, the comparison operators of PHP produce Boolean values. Analyze the following snippet:

$first_value = 3;

$second_value = 4;

```
if ($second_value > $first_value) {

    print "The second value is greater than the first one\n.";

}
```

Here, the system will check whether the condition is met. The result is a Boolean value (i.e. either true or false). If the conditional statement evaluates to true, the command included inside the curly braces will run.

Null

This data type can only have one value, which is "NULL." You will use this type to mark empty variables. If you are working with databases, you can use "Null" to differentiate invalid values and empty strings.

The isset() operator of this language gives false for Null values if the variable being checked exists. When used on other data types, however, isset() will give you true if the variable exists.

Resource

This is considered as a special type of data. It represents an extension resource of PHP such as an open file. Keep in mind that you won't handle a resource variable directly. Rather, you will simply send it to different functions that can interact with the involved resource.

Arrays

In the PHP language, an array is a group of value/key pairs: it indexes keys to their respective values. An array index can take the form of a string or integer while values can belong to any data type (even other arrays).

- *Declaring an Array* – You can use the array() construct when declaring an array. This construct requires the following syntax:

  array([key_to_be_used =>] value, [key_to_be_used =>] value, ...)

  In this syntax, the "key_to_be_used" entry is completely optional. If you won't specify the key, the system will automatically create one for you. The key will be the highest available integer plus one. PHP allows you to mix keyed and non-keyed arrays inside a single declaration.

- *Accessing an Array Element* - You need to use the $arr[key] syntax to access an array element. In this syntax, "key" can be a string or an integer. Make sure that you will include the quotation marks while using constant strings as keys (e.g. $arr["string"]. This syntax is extremely useful: you can use it to read existing elements or create new ones.

Constants

While using PHP, you can set names, known as constants, for basic values. Just like in other languages, you can't alter a PHP constant once you have assigned its value. The rules for naming a constant are almost identical to those used in naming a variable. The only difference is that a constant doesn't need a dollar sign before its name. When declaring constants, most programmers opt for uppercase letters. This approach helps them to achieve readability for their codes.

PHP allows you to access a constant at any part of your code. That means you don't need to declare them in each of your functions and PHP files. Here's the function that you should use when defining a constant:

define("NAME_OF_CONSTANT", value)

Where:

- "NAME_OF_CONSTANT" is a typical string that consists of letters and numbers.
- value is any PHP expression except objects and arrays.

The code snippet given below will show you how to define and use constants:

```
define("OK" 0);
define("ERROR", 1);

if ($errorcode == ERROR) {
  print("An error has occured\n");
}
```

Operators

The PHP language supports three kinds of operators: unary, binary and ternary.

A binary operator requires two operands. For example:

```
1 + 5
```

```
13 * 3.14
```

```
$x / 10
```

Keep in mind that you can only conduct a binary operation on values that belong to the same data type. If the operands you're working on have different data types (e.g. string and integer), the PHP language will perform automatic conversion. Thus, it will convert a data type to a different one to attain consistency. This automatic conversion works this way:

- If you are working with an integer and a floating-point number, the former will be converted to the data type of the latter.

- If you are dealing with a string and an integer, PHP will convert the former.

- If you're working on a real value and a string, PHP will convert the latter.

The Binary Operators

The Assignment Operators

An assignment operator allows you to assign values to your variables. Here, you should write the variable's name on the left-hand side of the expression. Place the value you want to assign at the right-hand side of the expression. For instance, in the expression $sample = 10, you will assign 10 to the variable named "sample."

Aside from "=", there are various assignment operators that you can use in PHP. These operators, which involve certain mathematical symbols, perform an operation and give the result to the left-hand operand. Here are some examples:

- *$counter += 1; /* In this expression, PHP will add 1 to the current value of the counter. Then, it will assign the sum as the new value of that variable. */*

- *$fund -= $expenses; /* Here, PHP will deduct the value of a variable named expenses from that of "fund" and assign the difference as the latter's new value. */*

PHP supports the following assignment operators:

=, -=, /=, *=, +=, .=, |=, >>=, <<=, &=, ^=, and &=

The Numeric Operators

In general, binary operators require numeric operands. If you are dealing with nulls, strings, resources, or Booleans, the system will convert the values to numbers before performing any calculation. Here are the numeric operators that you will find in PHP:

- "+" - This is called the "Addition" operator. It adds the values of two operands and returns the sum.

- "-" - Programmers refer to this as the "Subtraction" operator. It deducts the value of the right-hand operand from that of the left-hand operand and returns the difference.

- "*" - This is the "Multiplication" operator. It multiplies the values of two operands and returns the product.

- "/" - With this operator, you can divide the value of the left-hand operand by that of the right-hand operand and returns the quotient.

- "%" - This is the "Modulus" operator. It divides the value of the left-hand operand by that of the right-hand operand and returns the remainder.

The Concatenation Operator

This operator allows you to concatenate strings. Since it only works on string values, it converts non-string operands before doing any operation. The code snippet given below will give you "My favorite number is 23":

$favorite_number = 23;

print "My favorite number is " . $favorite_number;

The concatenation operator converts the integer $favorite_number to a string (i.e. "23") before combining the operands.

The Comparison Operators

You can use these operators to compare the values of two operands. If you are dealing with two string operands, PHP will perform the comparison in a lexicographical manner. Thus, it will give a Boolean result. The comparison operators listed below perform automatic data type conversions whenever necessary:

- "==" - This operator checks whether the operands have equal values. It will give you true if the values are equal. For example, "3 == 4" evaluates to false.

- "!=" - This is the exact opposite of the previous operator. It will give you true if the values inside the operands are not equal. For instance, "3 != 4" evaluates to true.

- ">" - With this operator, you can check whether the value of the left-hand operand is greater than that of the right-hand operand. If so, you will get true as the result. For instance, "3 > 4" will give you false.

- "<" - Use this operator to determine whether the left-hand operand's value is less than that of the right-hand operand. If it is, you will get true. For example, "3 < 4" evaluates to true.

- "<=" - Programmers refer to this as the "less than or equal to" operator. It will give you true if the value of the left-hand operand is less than or equal to the second operand. For example, "3 <= 4" will give you false.

- ">=" - This is the "greater than or equal to" operator. If the value of the left-hand operand is greater than or equal to that of the right-hand one, you will get true; otherwise, you will get false. For example, "3 >= 4" evaluates to false.

The Logical Operators

This kind of operator converts its operands to Boolean form before performing any comparison. Here are the logical operators that PHP supports:

- "&&" - This is called the "Logical AND" operator. It will give you true if both of the operands are true.

- "||" - Programmers call this the "Logical OR" operator. When used in PHP codes, it will give you true if at least one of operands is true.

- "xor" - This is the "Logical XOR" operator. It will give you true if only one of the operands is true. Thus, you will get false if both of the operands are true or false.

Important Note: The Logical OR and Logical AND operators allow short-circuit evaluation. That means they can give a result even without checking the entire expression. Logical OR, for example, will give you true if the first operand is true, since its condition has already been met (i.e. at least one of the operands should be true). The Logical AND operator, on the other hand, will give you false if the first operand is false. It won't check the second operand anymore since the assigned condition cannot be met no matter what (i.e. both operands should be true).

The Bitwise Operators

A bitwise operator conducts operations on the bitwise form of its operands. Unless the operands are strings, they will be converted to their respective binary form, and the operation will run. In situations where both of the operands are strings, PHP will perform the operation by matching character offsets (e.g. the system will treat the characters as binary numbers).

- "&" - This is the "Bitwise AND" operator. It will place 1 in each position where both operands have 1.

- "|" - This operator, known as Bitwise OR, places 1 in positions where at least one operand has 1.

- "^" - Programmers refer to this as the "Bitwise XOR" operator. It places 1 in each position where only one of the operands has 1.

The Unary Operators

Operators that belong to this type work on single operands.

The Negation Operators

These operators reverse the current value of its operand. PHP supports two negation operators, which are:

- "!" - Programmers call this the "Logical Negation" operator. It will give you true if the operand's value is false. If the value is true, on the other hand, this operator will give you false.

- "~" - This is the Bitwise Negation operator. It replaces 0 with 1, and vice versa.

The Increment and Decrement Operators

These operators have a unique characteristic – they work on a variable, not on the stored value. This is because aside from getting the result of an operation, they also change the value stored inside the variable. The PHP language supports two increment operators and two decrement operators. These are:

- $sample++ - This is the "Post-increment" operator. It returns the current value of the variable and increases it by 1.

- $sample-- - Programmers refer to this operator as "Post-decrement." Basically, this operator gives the current value of a variable before decreasing it by 1.

- $++sample – This operator, which is called "Pre-increment," increases the value of the variable it is attached to and returns the resulting value.

- $--sample – With this operator, you can decrease the value of an operand by one before retrieving an output.

The Cast Operators

PHP offers six cast operators that you can use to force type conversions. You should place the operator on the left-side of the operand. The list given below shows all of the cast operators in PHP:

- (array) – This operator changes the data type of a value to "array."

- (int) or (integer) – Use this operator to convert values into integers.

- (string) – This is the operator that you should use to create string values out of non-string ones.

- (object) – With this operator, you can tag any value as an "object."

- (real), (float) or (double) – This operator allows you to convert values from any data type into floating-point values.

- (bool) or (boolean) – Use this operator to convert any value into its Boolean form.

Keep in mind that a cast operator affects the value of a variable, not the variable itself. For instance:

$sample_string "10";

$sample_number = (int) $sample_string;

In this example, the variable named $sample_number gets the integer 10 as its value. The variable called $sample_string, however, still belongs to the string type.

The Ternary Operator

Programmers consider the question mark operator (i.e. ?) as one of the coolest operators of any language. In PHP, the format of this operator is:

conditional_statement ? first_expression : second_expression

The "?" operator evaluates the result of "conditional_statement." If the result is true, the operator will return the value of "first_expression." If the result is false, the operator will give you the value of "second_expression."

The code snippet given below will help you to understand how this operator works:

$x = 100;

$sample_message = isset($a) ? '$x exists' : '$x doesn't exist';

print $sample_message;

If you will run this code, your screen will print the following:

"$x exists"

Chapter 2: The Control Structures

This programming language supports the best control structures offered by other computer languages. PHP users divide control structures into two types: conditional control and loop control. A conditional control structure influences the program's flow and runs or skips certain codes based on predetermined criteria. A loop control structure, on the other hand, runs a piece of code multiple times according to the criteria set by the programmer. Let's discuss each type of structures in detail:

Conditional Structures

You need to use conditional statements when writing programs. These statements allow your programs to behave differently based on the user's inputs and their own "decisions." In PHP, you can use "if" statements and "switch" statements. These statements are two of the most popular control structures in computer programming.

The "if" Statements

This category consists of three statements, namely:

1. if (conditional_expression)

    statement/s

2. elseif (conditional_expression)

    statement/s

3. elseif (conditional_expression)

    statement/s

    ...

    else

      statements

These statements are considered as the most popular conditional constructs in programming and scripting. Actually, you'll find them in most computer languages. Each "if" statement has a conditional expression known as the "truth expression." If an "if" statement's truth expression results to true, the statement or group of statements under it will run; otherwise, they will be ignored.

You may place an "else" clause to your "if" statement to run codes only if the conditional expressions you have provided evaluates to false. Here's an example:

if ($sample >= 100) {

  print '$sample is within the given range';

  } else {

   print '$sample is invalid';

}

As you can see, curly braces define the statements under each "if" and "else" clauses, turning these statements into a "code block." In this example, you may remove the curly braces since each code block holds a single statement. However, it's still best if you will write braces in situations where they are completely optional. Braces improve the readability of PHP codes.

You can use an "elseif" construct to perform a sequence of conditional assessments and only run the code under the first satisfied condition. For instance:

if ($sample < 0 {

  print '$sample is a negative integer';

} elseif ($sample == 0) {

  print 'sample is equal to zero';

} elseif ($sample > 0 {

  print '$sample is a positive integer';

}

The "switch" Statement

The syntax of a switch statement is:

switch (expression) {

  case expression:

   statement/s

  case expression:

statement/s

...

default:

statement/s

}

Programmers use switch statements to replace complicated if-elseif statements. Switch statements compare an expression against all of the possible entries inside their body. If they don't find an exact match, the program will run the "default" clause and ignore the rest of the statement. In PHP, you may use a "break" statement to terminate the code's execution and pass the control to the succeeding scripts. Most programmers place the break statement at the last part of the switch structure. Analyze the following example:


```
switch ($solution) {
  case 'x':
  case 'x':
    print "The solution is correct\n";
    break;
  case 'u':
  case 'U':
    print "The solution is incorrect\n";
    break;
```

default:

print "Error: The system doesn't recognize the solution\n";

break;

}

The Loop Structures

You can use loop structures to repeat certain processes in your PHP scripts. For instance, you can use a "loop" to submit the results of a query multiple times. In this part of the book, you'll learn about the loop structures supported by the PHP language:

The "while" Loop

When writing a "while" loop, you should use the following syntax:

while (expression)

statement/s

Most programmers consider "while" loops as the simplest type of loops in any language. At the start of each repetition, the program will evaluate the loop's truth expression. If the expression's result is true, the loop will run all the statements inside it. If the result is false, however, the loop will end and pass the program control to the statements after it.

The "break" and "continue" Clauses

In PHP, "break" clauses and "continue" clauses require the following syntax:

break;

break expression;

continue;

continue expression;

There are times when you need to end the loop during an iteration. Because of this, PHP offers "break" statements. If a break statement appears as a single line (i.e. break;), the program will affect the innermost loop. You can specify the maximum levels you want to work on by setting an argument for your "break" clause. Here's the syntax:

break x;

The "do... while" Loop

This is the syntax that you should use while writing a "do... while" loop.

do

  statement/s

while (expression);

A "do... while" loop is like an ordinary "while" loop. The only difference is that a "do... while" loop checks its truth expression before ending each iteration. Basically, this kind of loop makes sure that your statement/s will run at least once, regardless of the truth expression's value.

Programmers use "do... while" loops to terminate code blocks upon satisfying a predetermined condition. Here's an example:

```
do {
  statement/s
  if ($sample) {
    break;
  } statement/s
} while (false);
```

Since a "do... while" loop run at least once, the statement or statements you place inside this loop will run once only. Additionally, the value of its truth expression always evaluates to false. PHP allows you to place break clauses inside a "do... while" loop to terminate its execution anytime. Obviously, you may use this kind of loop to facilitate typical reiteration processes.

The "for" Loop

The "for" loop of PHP is similar to that of the C language. This kind of loop takes three parameters:

for (start_expression; truth_expression; increment_expression)

Usually, programmers use a single expression for each part of the loop (i.e. truth, start, and increment). Thus, you can use the following syntax to create a basic "for" loop:

for (expression; expression; expression)

statement/s

The PHP interpreter evaluates the "start_expression" once. This expression initializes the control variable of the loop it belongs to. The element named "truth_expression", meanwhile, runs at the start of each loop iteration. All of the statements within the "for" loop will run if truth_expression evaluates to true; if it evaluates to false, the loop will end. The interpreter checks the increment_expression before ending each iteration. Programmers use the increment_expression to adjust the value of the loop's control variable.

You can include "continue" and "break" statements in your "for" loops. Keep in mind that "continue" forces the PHP interpreter to evaluate "increment_expression" before checking "truth_expression." The following example will show you how a "for" loop works:

```
for ($x = 0; $x < 5; $x++) {

  print "The square of this variable is " . $x*$x . "\n";

}
```

Just like C, PHP allows you to provide multiple expressions for each argument of the loop. You just have to delimit those expressions using commas. If you will use this option, each argument will take the value of its rightmost expression.

Additionally, you don't have to provide arguments for your "for" loops. The interpreter will just assume that the missing arguments evaluate to true. For instance, the code snippet given below will run continuously:

```
for ( ; ; ) {

  print "This loop is infinite\n";

}
```

The Code Inclusion Structures

You can use a code inclusion structure to organize the source of your programs. Aside from turning your complex codes into manageable blocks, a code inclusion structure can help you apply your codes on other PHP projects.

The "include" Statement

Just like other computer languages, PHP supports the usage of an "include" statement to divide codes into several files. Dividing your source code into different files is often useful for "code recycling" (i.e. using the same code on different scripts) or attaining code readability. Whenever you execute this statement, PHP will read a file, compile it into workable code, and run it.

The behavior of this statement is similar to that of a function. Keep in mind, however, that "include" is a pre-installed construct of the PHP language. When writing an "include" statement, you should use the following syntax:

include name_of_file;

The examples given below will show you how to write an "include" statement:

- *error_files.php*

```php
<?php

    $system_ok = 1;
    $system_error = 0;

?>
```

- check.php

```php
<?php

    include "error_files.php";

    print ('The variable named $system_error holds ' . "$system_error\n");
?>
```

If you will run this script, your screen will show you the following message:

"The variable named $system_error holds 0"

The eval() Function

This function is similar to the "include" statement. However, rather than compiling and running codes from a PHP file, it treats codes as basic strings. This feature can help you run dynamically generated codes or manually retrieve codes from external sources. You should know that using eval() is more complex than writing codes manually. Thus, it would be best if you'll avoid using this function.

Chapter 3: The Functions of PHP

PHP supports built-in and user-defined functions. All PHP functions respond to the following call:

func (argument_1, argument_2, argument_3, ...)

The arguments that you can include in a call depends on the function you're using. You may use any PHP expression as an argument. Actually, you can also tag other function calls as arguments. Here is one of the built-in functions of this language:

$sample = strlen("elephant");

The strlen() function accepts a string and returns its length. Thus, the variable named $sample will get 8 as its length, since "elephant" is eight characters long.

The User-Defined Functions

This is the syntax that you should use while defining a function:

function   name_of_function   (argument_1,   argument_2, argument_3, ...)

{

  statement/s

44

```
}
```

You can retrieve values from your functions by invoking the "return" expression inside them. By doing this call, you will stop the function's execution and get an immediate value. The example given below will show you how to define a function:

```
function square ($a)

{

  return $a*$a;

}
```

The Scope of a Function

Each function has a unique collection of variables. The variables you will define outside the definition of a function are inaccessible while you are inside the function. Once you run a function, you will also define its parameters. Using a new variable within the function defines that variable inside that function only. Additionally, that variable will disappear as soon as the function that contains it ends. The code snippet given below will illustrate this idea:

```
function example()

{

  $favorite_number = 1;

}
```

```
$favorite_number = 3;

example();
```

```
print $favorite_number;
```

Once you call the example() function, the variable named $favorite_number inside it won't affect the variable declared outside the function. Thus, this snippet will print "3" on your screen.

You probably want to know how you can access and/or modify $favorite_number from outside the function. As mentioned in the first chapter, you may use the pre-installed array called $GLOBALS[] to access any variable inside your script. You can rewrite the script given above as:

```
function example();
```

```
{
  global $favorite_number;
  $favorite_number = 1;
}
```

```
$favorite_number = 3;
```

example();

print $favorite_number;

With this code, your screen will display "1."

Additionally, the global keyword allows you to define which global variable/s you like to access. If you will use this feature, the system will import the global variable/s you selected to the scope of your function.

The "By Value" Method of Returning a Value

You can use a "return" statement to get values from your functions. This kind of statement returns a value "by value." Basically, it creates a copy of the appropriate value and sends it to the user. Here's an example:

function sample_function($test)

{

* return $GLOBALS[$test];*

}

$numeral = 4;

$sample_value = sample_function("numeral");

print $sample_value;

You will get "4" if you will run this code snippet. However, altering the $sample_value variable before "print" will affect that variable only. The changes that you will make won't affect $test, which is a global variable.

The "By Reference" Method of Returning a Value

In PHP, you can also use a reference to return values. That means you won't get a copy of the variable involved. Rather, you will get the address of that variable. This feature allows you to modify any variable from the call's scope. To use this method, you need to place "&" before the name of the function and within the invoker's code. The following example will show you how this method works:

```
function &sample_function($fruit)

{

  return $GLOBALS[$fruit];

}


$favorite_number = 5;

$sample_value =& sample_function("favorite_number");

print $sample_value . "\n";

$sample_value = 10;

print $favorite_number;
```

If you will run the code given above, your screen will display these numbers:

5

10

You were able to modify $favorite_number using $sample_value since the latter is an active reference to the former.

Important Note: Programmers rarely use this method. That's because it is inherently complex and often leads to bugs.

How to Declare a Function Parameter

PHP doesn't have a limit in terms of the number of arguments that you can assign to a function. In this language, you can pass arguments using two different approaches. The first one, known as "passing by values," is the most popular. Programmers refer to the second method as "passing by references." You should specify the method that you want to use while defining the function. Indicating the method during a function call will result to runtime errors.

The By-Value Parameters

This method accepts any PHP expression. Here, the program will evaluate the assigned expression and assign its value to a variable inside the function. For instance, in the example given below, $a gets 6 as its value while $b gets the value of another variable:

function sample($a, $b)

{

  ...

}

sample(2*3, $x);

The By-Reference Parameters

In this method, you need to use variables as arguments. Rather than passing the variable's actual value, a variable inside the function refers straight to the selected argument whenever activated. Thus, any modification done on the variable within the function will also affect the variable outside the function's scope. Here's an example:

function sample(&$a)

{

  $a = $a*$a;

}

$favorite_number = 5;

sample ($favorite_number);

print $favorite_number;

The ampersand sign before $a inside the function's parameter requires PHP to use the by-reference method. If you will run this code snippet, your screen will show "25."

The Default Parameters

A default parameter allows you to set default values for your functions. Thus, your functions will get a parameter automatically if you won't assign one. In the PHP language, you need to use constant values while setting default parameters.

Here's an example:

```
function increase(&$number, $sample = 5)
{
  $number += $sample;
}

$number = 1;
increase ($number);
increase ($number, 2);
```

The Static Variables

Similar to C, the PHP language supports the declaration of static variables. Static variables stay as they are between function invocations. However, you can only use them inside the function that contains them. You can initialize a static variable. The initialization process will take place once the program reaches the variable's declaration.

The following code snippet will show you how to declare a static variable:

```
function something_useful()

{

  static test = true;


  if (test) {
    // Run this code once the function is invoked.


    ...
  }



  // Run the main logic of the function each time this function is invoked.


  ...


}
```

Chapter 4: Object-Oriented Programming

This chapter will focus on the object-oriented style of programming. It will teach you the fundamentals of the object-oriented model. Additionally, it will provide you with detailed instructions on how to create and control objects. Study this material carefully if you want to be a skilled PHP user.

Objects – The Basics

In OOP (i.e. object-oriented programming), you will combine codes and data to create an object. A computer application created using this style consists of different objects that can communicate with each other. Often, these objects are self-contained and possess different methods and properties.

Properties serve as an object's data. Thus, these are variables owned by the object they point to. The methods, on the other hand, are functions an object supports.

Classes serve as templates for a programming object. They describe the properties and methods that an object will possess. In the example given below, the class describes a vehicle. For each vehicle inside your computer program, you may create an instance of the class to represent that vehicle's data. For instance, if two vehicles in your application are named "Car" and "Motorcycle," you will create two instances of your class and initialize the appropriate variable for each vehicle.

To initialize the variables, you need to invoke the method named setName() for the two vehicles. The members and methods that interacting objects can utilize are known as the "contract" of the class. For the example below, the car's contracts are the "get" and "set" methods, getType() and setType().

```
Class Vehicle {

  private $type;

  function setType ($type)
  {
    $this→type = $type;
  }
  function getType()
  {
    return $this→type;
  }
};

$car = new Vehicle();
$car→setType ("Car");

$motorcycle = new Vehicle();
$motorcycle→setType ("Motorcycle");
```

print $car→getType() . "\n";

print $motorcycle→getType . "\n";

Class Declarations

In PHP, declaring your own classes is easy and simple. You'll just type the word "class," specify the name you want to use, and indicate all of the properties and methods that instances from this class will possess. The syntax that you should use is:

class YourClass {

  ... // Place the methods you want to use here.

  ...

  ... // Place the properties you want to use here.

  ...

}

Important Note: You probably noticed the keyword "private" while working on the previous example (i.e. *private $type*). This keyword informs PHP that only the methods inside the class can use $type. Because of this keyword, you need to use setName() and getName() to set or get the $type property.

Creating Class Instances

You need to use "new" (i.e. a PHP keyword) to create class instances. In the last example, you generated an instance of the Vehicle class using *$car = new Vehicle();*. One you run this statement, PHP will create a new object and give it all of the properties declared in your chosen class. Then, PHP will invoke the object's constructor in case you defined one. A constructor is a PHP keyword that "new" invokes automatically after generating a new object. You can use a constructor to perform automated initializations.

Important Note: PHP allows you to set an argument or a group of arguments to your constructors. While using this feature, you have to write the parameters inside the parentheses.

The Destructor Functions

A destructor function is the opposite of a constructor. Programmers call it to destroy an object (e.g. when references to an object no longer exist). However, since the PHP language frees all of the system resources upon ending each request, the usefulness of destructor functions is severely limited. You may utilize them to flush resources or to log data while destroying an object.

You can only invoke a destructor during the following situations:

1. You are executing your script and you have destroyed all of the references to an object

2. When the application has reached the end of your script and PHP terminates the request

The second scenario is complex since you will rely on objects that may no longer exist. That means you need to be careful when facing that kind of situation.

Defining destructor functions is as easy as typing "_destruct()" inside your PHP class. Here's an example:

```
class YourClass {
 function _destruct()
 {
   print " This code destroys a \"YourClass\" object";
 }
}
```

```
$sample_object = new YourClass();
$sample_object = NULL;
```

If you will run this script, your screen will show you the following message:

"This code destroys a YourClass object"

Here, once the program reaches $sample_object = NULL;, the only reference to that object disappears. This triggers the destructor method, which eliminates the object itself. It is important to note that the destructor will still run even if the final line doesn't exist. However, that will happen at the termination of the request.

Important Note: PHP doesn't guarantee an exact time for calling the destructor method. In some cases, the destructor might execute several statements after releasing the final reference to an object. Keep this fact in mind while writing your PHP scripts.

How to Use "$this"

While executing a method of an object, PHP will define a variable named "$this" automatically. This variable is a reference that points to the programming object involved. You can reference the properties and methods of an object further using "→" and "$this." For instance, you can use $this→type to access the $type property of your object. As you can see, you don't need to type the dollar sign before the property's name. This is also the technique that you should use to access a method. For example, to get a vehicle's method, you may type: $this→getType().

The Private, Protected, and Public Properties

Access protection and encapsulation of properties play an important role in object-oriented programming. The most popular object-oriented languages offer three keywords for access restriction: private, protected, and public.

While defining members in the class's definition, you should indicate the access modifier that you want to use before specifying the members themselves. The code snippet given below will show you how to use these access modifiers:

```
class YourClass {

  private $privateSample = "private sample";

  private $protectedSample = "protected sample";

  public $publicSample = "public sample";


  function yourMethod() {


    // This is an example.
  }
}


$newObject = new YourClass();
```

Let's discuss each modifier in detail:

- private – To access an object's private members, you need to be inside one of the methods of that object. You can't access these members while you are inside a method of derived objects. Since you can't "see" private properties while you're inside an inheriting class, two different classes can declare identical private properties.

- protected – A protected member is similar to a private one in that you can only access it from inside the method of an object. The only difference between these members is that a protected member is visible from an inheriting class. In this kind of situation, you need to use the $this variable to access the protected members.

- public – You can access a public member both from inside the object (i.e. using the $this variable) and outside the object (i.e. through $object→Member). These rules will apply if a different class inherits public members. Here, you can access the members both from inside the class's methods and outside its objects.

Programmers use the "public" modifier for member variables that they need to access from outside the methods of an object. These people use "private" for variables that must be kept inside the logic of an object. Lastly, they use the "protected" modifier for variables that are placed inside an object, but will be passed on to inheriting classes. The following example will illustrate these ideas:

class YourDatabaseConnection {

public $searchResult;

protected $databaseHostname = "127.0.0.1";

private $connectionID;

// This is an example.

}

class MyDatabaseConnection extends YourDatabaseConnection
*   {*

protected $databaseHostname = "192.168.1.1";

This example, although incomplete, shows the proper usage of each access modifier. Basically, the class involved handles database connections (e.g. database queries):

- The system stores the connection ID inside a "private" data member. That's because only the internal logic of the class needs access to this information.

- Here, the user of the YourDatabaseConnection class cannot see the database's hostname. The programmer may override this by inheriting the data from the original class and altering the assigned value.

- The user needs to access the result of his/her search. Thus, $searchResult must be a "public" variable.

The Private, Protected, and Public Methods

You can use access modifiers on the methods of an object. Here are the rules that you need to remember:

- private – You can call a private method inside any of the class's methods. Invoking this kind of method is impossible if you're dealing with inheriting classes.

- protected – Calling a "protected method" can be done inside a method of the class.

- public - You can call a "public method" anywhere you want.

Important Note: If you won't specify an access modifier, PHP will tag your methods and properties as "public." Because of this, most of the examples you'll see in later chapters won't have any access modifier.

The Static Properties

In PHP, you can use classes to declare properties. All of the instances of a class have their own copy of the class's properties. However, you can also assign static properties to your classes. Unlike a typical property, a static property is only available for the class that contains it. Because of this, programmers refer to a static property as a "class property." To define a static property, use the following syntax:

class YourClass {

  static $sampleStaticVariable;

  static $sampleInitializedStaticVariable = 1;

}

When accessing a static property, you should indicate its name as well as the class it belongs to. Here's the syntax:

YourClass: :$sampleInitializedStaticVariable++;

print MyClass: :$sampleInitializedStaticVariable;

Your screen will display "2" if you will run the script given above.

If you want to access a member located inside a method of the class, you may specify the property using the "self" prefix. This prefix tells PHP that you are referring to the method the property belongs to. Check the following syntax:

class YourClass {

  static $sampleInitializedStaticVariable = 1;

  function yourMethod()

  {

    print self: :$sampleInitializedStaticVariable;

  }

}

$object = new yourClass();

$object→ yourMethod();

This example will print "1" on your screen.

The Static Methods

PHP allows you to declare a method as static. Basically, a static method is only available for the class that contains it. You can't use the $this variable while dealing with this kind of method. Rather, you should use the "self" keyword. Since a static method isn't linked to any object, you may call it without generating an instance through the "name_of_class: :method()" syntax. You can also call it within an object's instance though "$this→method(). Analyze the following example:

```
class Printer {

  static function printMessage()

  {

    print "Hi, how are you?";

    self: :printTabHere();

  }


  static function printTabHere();

  {

    print "\t";

  }

}


Printer: :printMessage();
```

This example will print "Hi, how are you?" and a tab character on your screen. Although this example is a basic one, it shows that you can call a method (i.e. printMessage()) inside the class even if there's no instance with the class's name. Additionally, this example shows how you can use a static method to trigger another method.

The Class Constants

PHP users have used global constants for a long time now. You can define a global constant using "define()", which you've studied back in the first chapter of this book. The current version of PHP supports enhanced encapsulation and the definition of constants within classes. Just like a static member, a class constant belongs to the class itself. This kind of constant is 100% case-sensitive.

The script given below will show you how to declare and access a class constant:

class ColorEnumeration {

  const YELLOW = "Yellow";

  const ORANGE = "Orange";

  const PINK = "Pink";

  function showPink()

  {

print self: :PINK;

  }

}

print ColorEnumeration: :YELLOW;

$object = new ColorEnumeration();

$object→showPink();

This example demonstrates the technique of accessing a class constant both from within a method (i.e. using "self") and through the class's name (i.e. ColorEnumeration).

Keep in mind that you can't change or remove a constant once you have defined it. Programmers use constants while working on enumerations or configuration values. In these situations, storing data permanently is a must.

Cloning an Object

While generating a new object, the resulting value serves as the handle or identification number of an object. The following code will illustrate this idea:

class YourClass {

  public $sample_variable = 2;

```
}
```

$object_1 = new YourClass();

$object_2 = $object_1;

$object_2→sample_variable = 3;

print $object_1→sample_variable;

Because $object_1 is a handle of an object, $object_2 will become another handle. Thus, if you will change the latter, you will change the object these variables are pointing to. If you will run the script given above, your screen will show you "3."

In some cases, you really need to copy an object. How do you accomplish this task? In PHP, you need to use the "clone" construct. This pre-installed opemethodrator generates an instance of an object automatically. The new instance will have all of the properties of the original object. Additionally, you may use the _clone() method to perform changes on the new object.

Important Note: Copying a reference results to another reference. You won't get an "in-depth" copy from that approach. That means if you will copy a reference that points to a different variable, the resulting object will also point to that variable.

Polymorphism

According to some people, polymorphism is one of the most crucial aspects of object-oriented programming. Describing real-life situations has become simple because you can use inheritance and classes in your codes. PHP codes are not just simple collections of data and functions. Polymorphism can do a lot of things for you. For example, it can help you complete projects by reusing codes or write powerful programs with minimal control statements. Analyze the following example:

```
class Dog {

 function arf()

 {

  print "arf";

 }

}


class Bird {

 function tweet()

 {

  print "tweet";

 }

}


function giveTheSound($object)
```

```
{
  if ($object instanceof Dog) {
    $object→arf();
  else if ($object instanceof Bird) {
    $object→tweet();
  } else {
    print "The object is invalid";
  }
  print "\n';
}


giveTheSound (new Dog ());
giveTheSound (new Bird());
```

If you will run this script, you will see the following message on your screen:

arf

tweet

Let's assume that you need to extend the previous example by adding more animals. You'll med to create an "else if" block for each new animal. Thus, you'll make a new instance of those animals and write more statements to invoke their sounds.

Polymorphism can simplify the task given above. Basically, this feature allows you to pass the contents of a class to other classes. Here, you can pass the properties and methods of a class to the new classes you want to create.

At this point, you need to create a class, name it "Animals", and establish relationships between this parent class and its specific objects. You can perform this inheritance by typing "extends" (i.e. another PHP keyword). Here's the syntax:

class ChildClass extends ParentClass {

  ...

}

Let's use "inheritance" to rewrite the code given earlier:

class Animals {

 function giveSound()

 {

 print "The program must re-implement this method in the inheriting classes.";

 }

}

```
class Dog extends Animals {
  function giveSound()
  {
    print "arf";
  }
}


class Bird extends Animals {
  function giveSound()
  {
    print "tweet";
  }
}


function rightSound($object)
{
  if ($object instanceof Animals) {
    $object→giveSound();
  } else {
    print "The object is invalid";
  }
  print "\n"
```

rightSound (new Dog ());

rightSound (new Bird ());

You'll get the following output:

arf

tweet

With this approach, you don't have to alter "rightSound()" regardless of the number of animals you want to add to the code. That's because "instanceof Animals" covers any animal that you might add.

Chapter 5: How to Handle Exceptions

Programmers consider exception handling as the most difficult part of software development. In general, errors (e.g. network failure, database failure, program bug, etc.) pose serious problems to program developers. For instance, developers need to make decisions regarding the errors that occurred, insert checks to prevent failure, and invoke the right function to manage it. Additionally, programmers need to make sure that their program will work as normal after handling the error.

Currently, most computer languages offer their own version of "try/catch/throw" (i.e. a popular paradigm for handling exceptions). The construct named "try/catch" protects the code it belongs to and informs the computer language about its security tasks. Here, the program will "throw" errors and exceptions as soon as they are detected. Then, the language (e.g. PHP) will scan its execution stack to know whether there's a "try/catch" construct that can handle the problem.

This method offers a lot of advantages. For example, it allows you to write robust programs without having to write "if" statements in each of your code blocks. That means you can minimize the codes that you need to write. With the "try/catch/throw" paradigm, you can just enclose code blocks with "try/catch" constructs and manage errors once they occur. Moreover, upon detecting an exception via the "throw" construct, you may go back to a part of the code that can handle and continue the program's execution.

The "try/catch" construct requires the following syntax:

try {

   ... // The code block which might encounter exceptions.

} catch (ExceptionClass1 $sample_exception) {

   ... // The code you want to use to handle the exception/s.

} catch (ExceptionClass2 $sample_exception) {

}

You need to place your PHP codes inside "try{}." As you can see, this construct precedes a collection of "catch" clauses, each defining what exception it will handle and what name should be used for identifying the errors.

When the program throws an exception, the initial catch() statement will run and PHP will compare the "instanceof" of the code and the specified class. If this comparison results to true, PHP will enter the "catch" code block and make the exception available under the specified variable identifier. If the comparison results to false, however, PHP will check the succeeding catch statement. The language's engine will check for other "try/catch" blocks if there's no relevant catch statement in the current construct.

Here's the syntax of a "throw" statement:

throw <name_of_object>;

This language doesn't allow you to throw basic data types (e.g. integers). Actually, PHP offers a built-in class for exceptions which is named "Exception." All of your exception classes should inherit from this pre-defined class. If you will try to throw objects that are not linked to the "Exception" class, your program will get runtime errors.

The code snippet given below will give you more information about the Exception class:

class Exception {

  function <u>construct</u> ([$theMessage [,theCode]]);

  final public getInfo();

  final public getCodes();

  final public getFiles();

  final public getLines();

  final public getTraces();

  final public getTracesAsStrings();

  protected $messages;

  protected $codes;

  protected $files;

  protected $lines;

}

The following code shows you how to write a complete "try/catch/throw" block:

```
class NullHandle extends Exception {
  function _construct ($sample_message)
  {
    parent: : construct ($sample_message);
  }
}


function printObjects ($object)
{
  if ($object == NULL) {
    throw new NullHandle ("The program received a NULL object.");
  }
  print $object . "\n";
}


class YourName {
  function _construct ($sampleName)
  {
    $this→sampleName = $sampleName;
```

```
}

function _toThisString()
{
  return $this→sampleName;
}


  private $sampleName;
}

try {
  printTheObject (new YourName ("John"));
  printTheObject (NULL);
  printTheObject (new YourName ("Mary"));
} catch (NullHandle $sample_exception) {

  print $sample_exception->getMessages();
  print " in the file " . $sample_exception->getFiles();
  print " on the line " . $sample_exception→getLines() . "\t";
} catch (Exception $sample_exception) {
  // The program won't reach this part.
}
```

Important Note: Follow these rules while using exceptions:

1. Keep in mind that an exception is an exception. You must only utilize it to manage problems.

2. Don't use an exception to control the flow of your program. Doing so makes source codes overly complex.

3. The data inside an exception should be limited to things related to the error. This must not involve any parameter (or extra information).

Chapter 6: The Advanced Concepts of Object-Oriented Programming

This chapter will teach you the advanced concepts and capabilities of object-oriented programming. Read this material carefully if you want to learn PHP in just 24 hours.

The Overloading Capabilities of OOP

In the PHP language, C-based programming extensions can overload the entire syntax of object definitions. PHP codes, on the other hand, can only overload certain subsets of the object syntax. In this part of the book, you will learn about the overloading features that you can use with PHP:

How to Overload Methods and Properties

This language allows you to overload method calls and property access. You can achieve these things through special methods that will run if the related method or property doesn't exist. That means you have lots of flexibility in terms of declaring your own functionalities and stopping these actions.

Here are the method prototypes that you can implement in PHP:

function _get ($propertyName)

function _set ($propertyName, $sampleValue)

function _call ($sampleMethod, $arguments)

Let's discuss each prototype in detail:

- "_get" - This method takes the name of a property. Use this prototype to return values.

- "_set" - You can pass the value and name of a property to this method prototype.

- "_call" - With this prototype, you can pass the name of a method and an indexed array.

The code given below will show you how to use the _get and _set functions:

```
class CoordinateClass {

  private $array = array ('a' => NULL, 'b' => NULL);


  function _get ($sampleProperty)
  {
    if (array_key_exists ($sampleProperty, $this→array)) {
      return $this→array [$sampleProperty];
  } else {
    print "The system can't read properties aside from a and b\n";
  }
}
```

```
function _set ($sampleProperty, $sampleValue)
{
  if (array_key_exists ($property, $this→array)) {
    $this→array[$sampleProperty] = $sampleValue;
    } else {
      print "The system can't write properties aside from a and b\n";
    }
  }
}


$object→a = 10;
print $object→a;


print "\n";


$object→e = 20;
print $object→e;
```

If you will run this script, you will get the following output:

10

The system can't read properties aside from a and b

The system can't write properties aside from a and b

Since "a" exists inside the array of the object, the get and set method handlers can read/write the right values. However, while accessing "e", both for writing and reading, array_key_exists() will give your false. Thus, the program will reach the assigned error messages.

You can use the _call() prototype for a wide range of purposes. In the following example, you will know how to generate a delegation scheme:

```
class HiClass {
  function show($sampleCount)
  {
    for ($a = 0; $a < $sampleCount; $a++) {
      print "Hi, how are you?\n";
    }
    return $sampleCount;
  }
}

class HiDelegator {
  function _construct()
```

```php
{
    $this→object = new HiClass();
}


function _call ($sampleMethod, $sampleArguments)
{
    return    call_user_func_array(array    ($this→object    ,
$sampleMethod) ,

    $sampleArguments;
}


    private $sampleObject;
}


$sampleObject = new HiDelegator();
print $sampleObject→show(5);
```

If you will run this script, your screen will show you:

Hi, how are you?

Hi, how are you?

Hi, how are you?

Hi, how are you?

Hi, how are you?

5

The function named "call_user_func_array()" allows the "_call()" prototype to pass the call and arguments to HiClass: :show(). Aside from relaying a call to another object, you may also return values from the _call() method prototype.

How to Overload the Syntax of Array Access

Often, programmers have value or key mappings (also known as "lookup dictionaries") in their program framework. This is the reason why PHP offers associative arrays. Basically, associative arrays map string and integer values to other PHP-supported values. You've learned about it in a previous chapter. To help you remember this concept, here's a code snippet that uses an array to search for a user's SSN:

print "Mike's SSN is " . $sampleMap ["Mike"];

Associative arrays become extremely useful if the user has all of the information needed. However, if you are dealing with millions of database entries, loading the whole database to the $sampleMap associative array to search for a single user is impractical. Here, you should create a new method that can search for the person's SSN through a database invocation. You can use this approach to rewrite the code snippet given above. The new code will look like this:

print "Mike's SSN is " . $database→LocateSSN ("Mike");

This approach works perfectly. However, many programmers opt to use the associative syntax when accessing value/key dictionaries. Because of this, PHP allow you to overload objects so they behave like typical arrays. You can use the syntax of associative arrays, but actually, PHP will call a method you wrote, which will run the appropriate database invocation and retrieve the needed data.

The method you want to use for accessing value/key dictionaries is up to you. In some cases, it is better to utilize the overloading capability of PHP than to invoke methods through verbose codes. In the end, the method that you should use depends on your needs and preferences.

The Iterators

You can use the foreach() loop to iterate an object's properties. Here's an example:

```
class YourClass {
    public $personName = "Mike";
    public $personSex = "male";
}


$object = new YourClass();


foreach ($object as $sampleKey => $sampleValue) {

    print "object [$sampleKey] = $sampleValue\n";
}
```

This script prints the following message:

```
object [sampleName] = Mike
object [sampleSex] = male
```

While writing object-oriented scripts, however, your class might not represent a basic array like the one given above. Your code might contain complex information, such as configuration files or database queries.

The PHP language lets you overload the foreach() iteration's behavior inside your code. That means you can use foreach() statements according to the needs of your program.

The Design Patterns

You'll encounter certain problems while designing your programs. Expert programmers have addressed and solved some of these problems, known as "design patterns." Basically, design patterns provide programmers with a common approach to program design. You've probably heard application developers say, "This project requires the singleton scheme." In this part of the book, you'll learn about the most important design patterns. Read this material carefully – it will help you learn PHP in just 24 hours.

The Strategy Pattern

Programmers use this pattern when they need an algorithm that can be interchanged with different variants. For instance, if your code generates an image, you might want to generate GIF files now and JPEG ones later.

Often, programmers implement this pattern by declaring a base class using an algorithm-based method. The program will implement this method by inheriting one or more concrete classes. Somewhere inside the code, the programmer will decide which concrete strategy must be used. PHP will substantiate that strategy and use it wherever appropriate.

The example given below shows how download servers can choose a file selection scheme based on the web browser that accesses them. While generating the HTML containing the download buttons, it will generate links to .zip or .tar.gz files based on the OS (i.e. operating system) identification of the web browser. To keep things simple, assume that when "Win32" exists in $_server["HTTPS_USER_AGENT"], you are working with a Windows computer and need to generate .zip download links; otherwise, you're working with a computer system that needs .tar.gz links.

This example involves two different strategies: .zip and .tar.gz. Analyze the following code: it will show you how to write effective strategy patterns:

```
abstract class FileSelectionStrategy {

  abstract function generateLink ($nameOfFile);

}


class ZipStrategy extends FileSelectionStrategy {

 function generateLink ($nameOfFile)

 {

   return "https://downloads.samplesite.com/$nameOfFile.zip";

 }

}


class TarGzStrategy extends FileSelectionStrategy {
```

```php
function generateLink ($nameOfFile)

{

  return
"https://downloads.samplesite.com/$nameOfFile.tar.gz";

 }

}


if (strstr($_SERVER ["HTTPS_USER_AGENT"], "Win32")) {

  $selectionObject = new ZipStrategy();

} else {

  $selectionObject = new TarGzStrategy();

}


$mark_filename = $selectionObject→generateLink
("Marketing101");

$sales_filename = $selectionObject→generateLink ("Sales101");


print <<<EOF

<h1>These free eBooks will help you become a better
entrepreneur</h1>

<br>

<a href="mark_filename">An eBook that focuses on
marketing</a><br>

<a href="sales_filename">An excellent resource for sales-related
concerns</a><br>
```

*
*

EOF;

If you will access this script using a Windows machine, you'll get the following output:

<h1>These free eBooks will help you become a better entrepreneur</h1>

<a href="https://downloads.samplesite.com/Marketing101.zip">An eBook that focuses on marketing<a>

<a href="https://downloads.samplesite.com/Sales101.zip>An excellent resource for sales-related concerns</a>

6.3.2 The Singleton Pattern

This is one of the most popular patterns in software design. Programmers often encounter situations where they have objects that handle certain centralized operations in the program (e.g. logger objects). In these situations, programmers prefer to keep things simple by creating a program-wide instance that can be accessed by any part of the source code. Particularly, when dealing with logger objects, you need each part of the application to access that instance, and allow the logging mechanism/s manage log messages based on log level configuration. The singleton design pattern is your best bet when facing this kind of situation.

You can convert your classes into singleton classes by implementing "getInstance()". Basically, "getInstance()" is a static method that returns the lone instance of a class. If you will invoke this method for the first time, it will generate an instance, save that in a static variable, and return that instance to you. Subsequent calls to the "getInstance()" method returns the handle of the instance created before. Analyze the following example:

```
class SampleLogger {

  static function getInstance()

  {

    if (self: :$sampleInstance == NULL) {

      self: :$sampleInstance = new SampleLogger();

    }

    return self: :$sampleInstance;
```

```
    }

    private function _construct ()
    {
    }

    private function _clone ()
    {

    }

    function Log ($sampleString)
    {
        // This code takes care of log-related processes.
    }

    static private $sampleInstance = NULL;
}


sampleLogger: :getInstance () →Log ("Check");
```

The important part of this code is "sampleLogger: :getInstance ()". This part allows you to access the "logger" from any part of your code.

For this application,"clone" and "constructor" are tagged as private methods. This approach makes sure that the programmer won't create another instance of the sampleLogger class mistakenly. Simply put, "getInstance()" serves as the only way for you to access an instance of the class.

The Factory Pattern

In object-oriented programming, polymorphism and base class utilization play important roles. Base classes contain subclasses, which sometimes require the creation of concrete instances. In PHP, programmers use a design pattern called "factory" to create the needed subclasses. Factory classes have a method that takes an input. Depending on the input provided, these classes will decide what kind of instance to generate (often a subclass).

Let's assume that your website allows different types of users to sign in. Some of these people are visitors, some are customers, and some are administrators. In this situation, most programmers will create a base class and three subclasses. You may name the base class as "Users." Then, you may name the subclasses as "Visitors," "Customers" and "Admins." The base class and all of its subclasses will contain methods that can collect data regarding the user (e.g. the user's personal preferences and the online resources he/she can access).

You can create a robust website by using the "Users" base class whenever you can. This way, you can generalize your source code and simplify the addition of new user types.

The Observer Pattern

Programs created using PHP manipulate information. In most cases, modifications done on a piece of information influence different sections of the program's source code. For instance, if a customer from Asia visits the U.S. section of eBay, exchange rates will affect the prices that he/she will see on his screen.

Let's assume that each programming object represents one eBay product. The objects used in the code come straight from eBay's database. The exchange rates, on the other hand, will likely come from an external data source and are not saved in the database. Each object contains "display()", a method that returns the HTML content related to the product.

The "observer" design pattern allows objects to sign up for specific information and/or events. When the information gets changed or an event happens, PHP will notify the registered objects. With this approach, you can tag a product item as an observer of the exchange rate. Additionally, you may update the registered programming objects about the exchange rates prior to printing out item lists. That means each object can update itself and include the new information in its display() method.

Often, PHP users implement observer patterns through an interface known as the "observer." Classes that need to act as observers should implement this interface.

An "observable" object often has a method named "register," which lets the "observer" (i.e. the interface) to sign up automatically.

Chapter 7: Using PHP to Create an Application

People use PHP to build websites. This computer language allows programmers to make dynamic web applications. A dynamic application collects data from users through HTML forms. The data obtained from users and saved in the website is confidential, which makes security a serious concern. The PHP language has features that allow you to obtain and store data securely. PHP has everything you need: you just need to develop applications using the features offered by this language. In this chapter, you'll learn how to use PHP in building dynamic web applications.

PHP and HTML

You don't have to embed PHP codes into HTML files. You can always produce PHP files that don't contain any HTML element. When creating web applications, however, you will likely combine these languages in a single file. Computer experts say that PHP was created for websites, to be used as a template for HTML documents. Once you add PHP into a file, that file will get ".php" or ".php5"as its extension.

The code given below shows how you can combine PHP and HTML:

<html>

<head><title>First Sample</title></head>

<body>

<?php

```
// This code has a data-based "if" statement.
if (date('md' == '1225')) {
  echo 'Merry Christmas '
   'and Happy New Year';
} else {
  echo 'Hi, how are you?';
}
?>
</body>
</html>
```

In this example, the "<?php" part signifies the start of the embedded PHP code. The "?>" part, on the other hand, indicates the end of the PHP code. You probably noticed that this example sends the output through "echo." This approach is acceptable if you are dealing with simple codes such as the one given above. However, if you are using "echo" on strings that have single/double quotes, your code will be extremely complicated.

This example will result to an error if the echoed text is a link (e.g. <a href='https...'>). That's because the quotes in the echoed text will be in conflict with the quotes that encloses the string. In this kind of situation, you may end the PHP part before processing the text's output. Then, start it again before the code that terminates the "if" statements. Here's an example:

```
<html>
```

```php
<head><title>Second Sample</title></head>
<body>
<?php
  // This code contains a date-based "if" statement.
  if (date('md' == '1225')) {
    echo 'Merry Christmas and ' .
      'Happy New Year!';
  } else {
    echo 'Hi, how are you?';
  }
?>
</body>
</html>
```

This style of writing codes is confusing. It violates an important programming principle: "Don't mix content and logic." The embedding style given below uses a variable to store the string and echoes that variable:

```php
<?php
  // This code contains a date-based "if" statement.
  if (date ('md' == '1225') ) {
    $message = 'Merry Christmas and Happy New Year!";
  } else {
```

97

```php
    $message =  'Hi, how are you?';

 }
?>
```
```html
<html>
<head><title>Third Sample</title></head>
<body>
<?php echo $message; ?>
</body>
</html>
```

Users' Input

After learning how to include PHP in an HTML file, you should know how to set user-specified actions. For example, an online bookstore requires a registration and login system. Obviously, users need to perform an action (e.g. enter login credentials) to get "inside" the online shop. This type of system needs HTML-based forms and a storage to keep the collected data in.

For this example, you need several things from each user during the registration process. These are: name, password and email address. Analyze the following HTML code:

```html
<html>
<head><title>Sign up</title></head>
<body>
```

```
<h1>Register Here</h1>
<form method="get" action="signup.php">
  <table>
  <tr><td>Email Address:</td>
    <td><input type='text' name='email address'/> </td></tr>
  <tr><td>Name:</td>
    <td><input type='text' name='first_last_name'/></td></tr>
  <tr><td>Desired Password:</td>
    <td><input type='password' name='desiredpassword'/></td></tr>
  <tr>
    <td colspan ='3'>
    <input type='submit' name='signup' value='Sign up'/>
    </td>
  </tr>
  </table>
 </form>
</body>
</html>
```

How to Handle User Input Safely

Don't trust anyone, particularly the people who use your website. People do unexpected stuff, whether by accident or on purpose. That means they might discover bugs or vulnerabilities in your website. This part of the book will discuss the problems that might happen to your site. Then, it will discuss the techniques that you can use to solve such problems.

Common Errors

Programmers make mistakes sometimes. If you will subscribe to security-related email lists, you will discover new weaknesses of PHP programs each week. Let's discuss some of the most popular errors related to PHP:

- Global Variables – In some cases, program developers fail to initialize global variables correctly. You can prevent this mistake by setting the 'register_globals' directive to "off." However, this problem can still occur so you need to be careful. Users whose register_globals are on might abuse your website application. For example, customers might gain admin-level access to your system just by running arbitrary codes on your site.

- Cross-Site Scripting – A hacker might use "cross-site scripting" to run client-side languages (e.g. JavaScript) to steal cookies and confidential information. This scripting technique is easy and simple. The hacker just needs to enter raw information into the website's HTML.

- SQL Injection – This method requires the hacker to insert malicious codes into his/her database queries.

Securing Your Scripts

If you want to secure your PHP scripts, never trust your website users. This statement, although harsh, is the best advice that you can get regarding security. Aside from hacking your website, users might perform strange things accidentally. As the programmer, you must ensure that hacking attacks and user mistakes won't cause significant damage on your web application. The following list shows the best techniques that you can use in protecting your website:

- Validate Inputs – You can protect your website by validating all of the inputs sent by your users. That means you will check the data of your users' "get," "post" and cookies.

    The first thing you need to do is turn off the "register_globals" section of php.ini. Then, set the highest possible value on the part named "error_level". Basically, "register_globals" stops the tagging of the request information (e.g. session, post, get, etc.) as a global variable in your PHP script. The "error_level" part, on the other hand, will allow notifications for variables that were not initialized.

    The methods that you'll use depend on the types of input

you're dealing with. For example, if the parameters contained in the "GET" method should be integers, you may force these parameters to have that data type. With this technique, all non-integer values will become "0."

- 7.3.2.2 HMAC Security – Hackers usually tamper with the variables within a URL (e.g. for page redirects or links that forward parameters to the connected script). As the programmer, you need to prevent hackers from implementing their evil plans. You can use hashes to protect your website. Today, HMAC is the ideal solution for your hashing needs.

Programmers consider HMAC as an excellent validation algorithm. You should choose this over "home-brewed" algorithms. With HMAC, your text will undergo a two-step encryption procedure.

Sessions

In PHP, sessions allow a program to store data for the active "session" (i.e. one person who uses the program). Each session has an ID – you can use that piece of information to identify the sessions in your PHP applications. This language generates session IDs by collecting the IP address of the remote user, the time, and some additional random data. Then, it will encrypt the collected data using the MD5 algorithm. You can pass this ID to a cookie or add it to the URLs that the user will use for site navigation.

To keep your web application secure, you should require users to enable their cookies than pass session IDs using URLs. As you know, information sent through URLs might get saved in the

102

server's records or get discovered by hackers who monitor the site's traffic.

File Uploads

PHP has a file upload functionality that you can use to upload different types of materials (e.g. images). Since the web browser should do more things than just transmit "POSTs" with relevant information, you must utilize a special form for uploading files. Here's an example:

```
<form enctype="multipart/form-data" action="handle_img.php"
➡method="post">
    <input type="hidden" name="MAX_FILE_SIZE" value="16000" />
    Send this file: <input name="book_image" type="file" /><br />
    <input type="submit" value="Upload" />
</form>
```

This code has an attribute named "enctype." The "enctype" attribute informs the user's web browser to transmit a different kind of request. The request needed here doesn't contain "field=var&field2=var2." Rather, the request's syntax resembles a text-based email, with all of its parts serving as form fields.

How to Handle Uploaded Files

The array named "$_FILES" hold a set of data regarding each uploaded file. The handler code can use a file's name to access data about that file. The variable called $_FILES['book_image'] holds the following data for each uploaded file:

- name – This is the file's name when it was still in the uploader's local machine.

- type – This indicates the file's MIME (i.e. Multipurpose Internet Mail Extensions) type. A JPG image can have image/pjpeg or image/jpeg as its MIME type. All non-text files have their own MIME type.

- tmp_name – This data serves as the file's temporary name inside the file system of the web server. The PHP language will delete this data after completing the upload request. That means you should do something about the file's tmp_name within the code that takes care of the user's request (i.e. either transfer or delete it).

- error – This number represents the type of error that occurred (if any). You'll learn more about errors later.

- size - This part shows the total size of the file.

Sometimes, users experience errors while uploading a file. Most of these errors are linked to the uploaded file's size. In PHP, error codes have a matching constant. Here are the errors that you might encounter while using this language:

104

Error Code	Name of Constant	Definition
0	UPLOAD_ERR_OK	This error code states that the upload process was successful. The system didn't encounter any error.
1	UPLOAD_ERR_INI_SIZE	This code means the file you want to upload exceeds the maximum file size specified in php.ini.
2	UPLOAD_ERR_FORM_SIZE	The file you are working on exceeds the maximum file size set for the system. You can't rely on this code since users can fake the size of their files.
3	UPLOAD_ERR_PARTIAL	The process was unsuccessful. The file received by the server is incomplete.
4	UPLOAD_ERR_NO_FILE	This error code states that the user didn't upload any file.

Architecture

At this point, you should know how to organize the scripts in your applications. This book will focus on the most popular methods of organizing PHP codes. Read this material carefully: it will help you master the basics of PHP in just 24 hours.

The One Script Approach

With this approach, you will use a single script to   handle   the requests of all the pages in the website. Programmers usually use the index.php script to implement this kind of architecture. Here, you can add URL parameters (e.g. ?page=register) to pass different types of content. You shouldn't save all of your codes inside index.php. It would be best if you will use the index.php script to save the most important parts of your code.

One Script for Each Function

Programmers consider this as one of their best options when it comes to program architecture. With this approach, you won't use a primary script (like the one discussed above). Rather, you will store your functions inside different scripts and access them through their URL.

If you will use this approach, you won't have to maintain a huge script. The main disadvantage of this approach, meanwhile, is that you need to write the basic codes inside each script.

Keep Layout and Logic Separated

Regardless of the approach you're using, you should always separate the layout from your logic. PHP offers a lot of techniques to attain this. For example, you may use a templating engine.

Chapter 8: Databases and the PHP Language

Almost all PHP books deal with databases. Thus, the final chapter of this eBook will teach you important things regarding databases. You need to read this material carefully since you will surely use databases for your PHP applications.

This chapter will focus on MySQL, one of the leading database management systems in the world.

MySQL – The Basics

PHP and MySQL form a great team: they serve as the main tools for application developers. Since you are studying PHP, you will encounter (and use) MySQL on a regular basis. This is the main reason why this book will focus on this database management system.

In the following pages, you will learn about "mslqi" (i.e. MySQL Improved). This extension of MySQL comes with the latest versions of PHP.

More Information about MySQL

The Pros

- It is popular – MySQL possesses the largest market share in the database management industry. Almost all hosting service providers offer access to MySQL. Additionally, you can easily find reading materials about MySQL. That means you can get and learn this database management system quickly and easily.

- It is intuitive – Once you have established your MySQL database, managing your data becomes a straightforward process. An administrator should configure the initial access to a database. Thus, if you will share your database with other people, you need to give them access to MySQL first.

- It is free – This database management system is open-source. That means you can use it without shelling out any money.

The Con

- You might need to purchase a license – You should buy a commercial license if you're planning to bundle MySQL with any closed-source software.

Database Queries

MySQL supports two kinds of queries: (1) buffered queries and (2) unbuffered queries. Let's discuss these queries in detail:

Buffered Queries

A buffered query retrieves the result and stores it in the client-side machine. If the user will run subsequent queries, his/her requests will go through the memory of his local machine first.

The main advantage of a buffered query is that you can search inside it. That means you can control the row pointer inside the result set according to your needs (considering that the information is stored in the local machine). Its primary disadvantage, on the other hand, is that the results require extra memory.

Unbuffered Queries

An unbuffered query doesn't allow you to move its row pointer. Thus, you have to follow the exact sequence of the search results. The advantage offered by this query is that it doesn't require excessive storage space. You may collect and process data rows once your MySQL server begins to return them. While using the result of an unbuffered query, you should get all of the rows using "mysqli_fetch_row" or free them using "mysqli_free_result". Your server won't respond to your requests until you issue one of these commands.

The kind of query that you should use depends on your situation. An unbuffered query allows you to save lots of computer memory when working with a huge result set. If you don't need to sort the search results, you will be able to see the initial row of the results through PHP even if MySQL is still running the query. A buffered query is convenient since it offers a powerful search functionality. It can boost your productivity significantly. Since individual queries will get completed quickly, mysql will immediately drain the results and store them in the local machine rather than running the search while working on the PHP codes.

After using MySQL and analyzing your results, you will know which type of query you should use.

Important Note: You need to be careful when running an unbuffered query. Keep in mind that the server will ignore your requests until you fetch or free the current results. Thus, you need to issue either mysqli_fetch_row or mysqli_free_result before sending any command to the server.

Conclusion

I hope this book was able to help you to learn the basics of the PHP scripting language in just 24 hours. The codes, instructions, and explanations you've read in this book prepared you in using PHP for your own websites and applications. If you will apply the lessons you've studied in this book, you will become a skilled PHP user in no time.

The next step is to read more books about PHP and continue writing your own codes. Keep in mind that programming is a complex activity. You need to gain knowledge from different sources in order to be a good programmer. By reading more books and practicing your skills, you will be able to boost your programming abilities greatly.

I wish you the best of luck!

Robert Dwight

Printed in Great Britain
by Amazon